100
things you should know about
ENDANGERED
ANIMALS

100
things you should know about
ENDANGERED ANIMALS

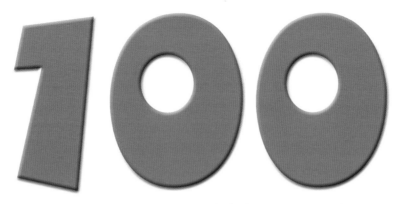

Steve Parker

BARNES & NOBLE

NEW YORK

Editorial Director: Belinda Gallagher
Art Director: Jo Brewer
Editorial Assistant: Sarah Parkin
Volume Designers: Simon Lee, Sophie Pelham
Picture Researcher: Lorraine King
Indexer: Gill Lee
Production Manager: Elizabeth Brunwin
Reprographics: Stephan Davies, Ian Paulyn

ACKNOWLEDGMENTS

The publishers would like to thank the following artists
who have contributed to this book:

Mike Foster, Mirella Monesi, Andrea Morandi, Eric Rowe, Mike Saunders

Cover artwork by Ian Jackson

All other artworks are from the Miles Kelly Artwork Bank

The publishers would like to thank the following sources for the use of their photographs:

Page 6 Frans Lanting/FLPA; 12(t) Jonathan & Angela Scott/NHPA, (b) Martin Harvey/Gallo Images/Corbis;
13 Art Wolfe/Getty Images; 14 Winfried Wisniewski/FLPA; 16(t) Save the Rhino International; 20 Frans Lanting/Corbis;
22 Fernando Bengaechea/Beateworks/Corbis; 23 Panda Photo/FLPA; 24(t) Karen Kasmauski/Corbis,
(b) Newman & Associates/Oxford Scientific; 25(t) Mark Carwardine/NHPA, (b) George Steinmetz/Corbis;
26(t) momatiuk-Eastcott/Corbis; 28(b) Jonathan & Angela Scott/NHPA; 29 Owen Franken/Corbis;
30 Luiz Claudio Marigo/naturepl.com; 31(b) Keren Su/Corbis; 32(t) Nick Gordon/PhotoLibrary,
(b) Karen Kasmauski/Getty Images; 33(t) Jeffrey L Rofman/Corbis, (b) Martin Harvey/NHPA;
34(t) Martin Wendler/NHPA, (b) Tui De Roy/Minden Pictures/FLPA; 35(t) Linda Lewis/FLPA,
(b) Andrew Murray/naturepl.com; 36 David Hosking/FLPA; 39 Flip Nicklin/Minden Pictures/FLPA;
40(t) David Hosking/FLPA, (b) Theo Allots/Corbis; 41 Martin Harvey/Corbis;
42 Katherine Feng/Globio/Minden Pictures/FLPA; 43(t) National Geographic/Getty Images,
(b) John F. Binns, www.IRCF.org; 44 Philip Perry/FLPA; 45 Yva Momatiuk & John Eastcott/Minden Pictures/FLPA;
46 Natalie Fobes/Corbis; 47 Theo Allots/Corbis

All other photographs are from:

Castrol, Corel, digitalSTOCK, digitalvision, John Foxx, PhotoAlto, PhotoDisc, PhotoEssentials, PhotoPro, Stockbyte

Made with paper from a sustainable forest

Barnes & Noble, Inc.,
122 Fifth Avenue
New York, NY 10011

www.mileskelly.net
info@mileskelly.net

ISBN-13: 978-1-4351-0521-8
ISBN-10: 1-4351-0521-4

Printed and bound in China

2 4 6 8 10 9 7 5 3 1

www.africanconservation.org
www.bornfree.org.uk

The publishers would like to thank the Born Free
Foundation and the African Conservation Foundation
for their help in compiling this book.

Contents

Animals in peril

1 Around the world, wild animals, plants, and the places they live in are disappearing fast. From the creatures of the rainforests to the animals that live in mountains, deserts, polar lands, and even in the oceans, countless numbers are under threat. Some animals have become so rare, they will die out forever. The main problem is that people are causing huge amounts of damage to the natural world. It is up to us to change our ways and save animals in danger.

▶ The biggest cat in the Americas, the jaguar is threatened by loss of its habitat. It is also shot or trapped by people in case it attacks their farm animals, their pets—or themselves.

Gone long ago

2 **In one sense, animals and plants have always been under threat.** It's part of nature's "struggle for existence." Creatures must find food, shelter, and other needs, and avoid predators and dangers. This has been happening for millions of years, as old types of living things died out, or became extinct, and new ones took over.

Saltasaurus

3 **About 65 million years ago, the dinosaurs died out, along with many other animals and plants.** This was a mass extinction, but it had nothing to do with people, because there were no humans then. Scientists are not sure why it happened, but the causes were natural. A huge asteroid may have smashed into the Earth. There have been many mass extinctions in the Earth's long history.

▲ The huge *Saltasaurus*, 39 feet long and weighing 8 tons, was one of the last dinosaurs. About 65 million years ago, it may have watched as a massive meteorite was about to smash into the Earth and cause the death of millions of animals and plants.

I DON'T BELIEVE IT!

More than 99 out of 100 kinds of animals that ever lived are now extinct— died out and gone for ever.

Pteranodon

4 Now there are humans on Earth, animals are becoming extinct at a faster rate than before. Wooly mammoths died out within the past 10,000 years. This may have been partly due to the end of the Ice Age, since they could not cope with warmer weather. However, being hunted by ancient people did not help.

Huge meteorite or asteroid

5 Many other large creatures have died out in the past few thousand years. These include cave bears, wooly rhinos, dire wolves, and giant deer. Some of these extinctions happened as people spread around the world.

Herd of *Edmontosaurus*

6 As the centuries passed, from ancient history to medieval times, more animals came under threat. The auroch was a huge wild cow, from which today's farm cattle were bred. It was hunted by people until it disappeared. The last auroch died in 1627, in a Polish forest.

◀ Wooly rhinos were well adapted to the cold with their long coats. Perhaps they could not cope as the Ice Age faded and the world warmed up. They too became extinct.

Too late to save

7 **In the last few hundred years, many kinds of animals have become endangered, and dozens have died out.** They include fish, frogs, snakes, birds, and mammals. Studying why these extinctions happened can help to save today's endangered animals.

8 **Being very common is no safeguard against human threats.** Five hundred years ago there were perhaps 5,000 million passenger pigeons. They were shot and trapped by people for their meat, and their natural habitats were taken over by crops and farm animals. The last passenger pigeon, "Martha," died in Cincinnati Zoo in 1914.

9 **A creature that went from discovery to extinction in less than 30 years was Steller's sea cow.** It was a huge, 3-ton cousin of the manatee and dugong, and lived in the Arctic region. It was first described by scientists in 1741. So many were killed in a short space of time, that Steller's sea cow had died out by 1768.

QUIZ

What died out when? Put these animals' extinctions in order, from most long ago to most recent.
A. Dodo
B. Blue antelope
C. Thylacine
D. Passenger pigeon
E. Steller's sea cow

Answers:
A E B D C

▶ The dodo has become a world symbol of extinction. Only a few bones, feathers, and bits of skin remain.

▲ Steller's sea cow was 26 feet long and almost as heavy as an elephant. However size was no protection, as its herds were slaughtered by sailors for meat, blubber, and hides.

11 The dodo, a turkey-sized bird with tiny wings that could not fly, was found on the island of Mauritius in the Indian Ocean. Sailors that stopped at the island captured dodos as fresh food. So many were killed that all dodos were extinct by 1700. This has led to the saying "as dead as a dodo."

▼ Every 7 September, Australia holds National Threatened Species Day. The day is in memory of the last thylacine that died on this date in 1936 at Hobart Zoo, in the state of Tasmania.

10 Many animals have became endangered, and died out forever. They include the blue antelope of Southern Africa (around 1800), the flightless seabird known as the great auk (1850s), the dog-like marsupial (pouched mammal) known as the thylacine or Tasmanian tiger (1936), and the Caribbean monk seal (1950s). The list is very long, and very sad.

How we know

12 **How do we know which animals are endangered and need our help?** Explorers and travelers bring back stories of rare and strange creatures. Sometimes they add bits to their tales to make them more exciting. Scientific studies and surveys are needed to find out which creatures are in trouble, and how serious the threats are.

▼ This lion, put to sleep briefly by a tranquillizer dart, is being tracked by its radio collar. Each lion has its own pattern of whisker spots, like a fingerprint, to help identify it.

▼ Rangers guard incredibly rare mountain gorillas, which soon get used to having them around. The rangers become well aquainted with the habits of the gorillas, which helps scientists carry out important research.

13 Firing a dart containing a knockout chemical makes a creature, such as a lion, sleep for a short time. Scientists then work fast to take blood samples, check for diseases, measure and weigh, and gather other useful information, before the animal wakes up.

14 Scientists need to know more than just how many individual animals are left in an endangered species. They try to find out the animals' ages, what they eat, how often they breed, how they move about or migrate, and how long they live. This all helps to build up knowledge of the species, and work out the best ways to take action.

▼ Aerial films and photographs can be studied to count big animals such as elephants, estimate their age, and work out if they are male or female.

15 Big animals in open habitats, such as elephants on the African savanna (grassland), are surveyed from the air. Planes, helicopters, and even balloons carry people who count the herds and take photographs.

16 It is extremely helpful to capture, tag, and release animals. Rare birds such as albatrosses are carefully caught in nets, and small rings are put on their legs. This helps scientists to identify each albatross every time it is seen. Tags in the ears of rhinos can work in the same way.

I DON'T BELIEVE IT!

When studying an endangered animal, one of the best things to have is—its poo! Droppings or dung contain much information about what a creature eats, how healthy it is, and any diseases it may have.

17 Some animals are big enough to attach a radio beacon to, which sends signals up to a satellite. Whales, sea turtles, seals, and other sea creatures can be tracked as they swim across the vast oceans.

How endangered?

18 We might suspect an animal is at risk, but how serious is the threat? The scientific organization called the IUCN, World Conservation Union, produces a "Red List" of threatened species of animals and plants. Each species is given a two-letter description to show its plight.

▲ The leafy sea dragon is threatened as it is caught by exotic fish collectors. It is also killed, dried, and powdered for the traditional medicine trade.

19 **NT is Near Threatened.** A species could be in trouble soon, but not quite yet. An example is the leafy sea dragon, a type of fish, whose flaps of skin make it look like swaying seaweed.

20 **VU is Vulnerable.** The species is already under threat, and help is needed over the coming years. An example is the northern fur seal, of the northern Pacific region.

◀ The northern fur seal was killed in large numbers for its thick, soft, warm fur, once used for coats.

► Cheetahs once lived across most of Africa and the Middle East, and were even partly tamed and kept as pets by royalty. They may disappear before long.

21 **EN is Endangered.** The species faces big problems and the risk of extinction over the coming years is high. An example is the cheetah, the fastest runner on Earth.

22 **CR is Critically Endangered.** This is the most serious group. Unless there is a huge conservation effort, extinction is just around the corner. An example is the vaquita, the smallest kind of porpoise, from the northern Gulf of California.

▲ Polluted water, drilling for oil and gas, and being caught in fishing nets are all deadly dangers for the 5-foot-long vaquita.

▼ Hawaiian crows are only found in captivity. Attempts to breed and release them have so far failed.

MATCH UP

Can you place these threatened creatures in their correct animal groups?

A. Whale shark   1. Bird
B. Spix macaw   2. Fish
C. Vaquita   3. Amphibian
D. Caiman   4. Mammal
E. Olm   5. Reptile

Answers:
A2 B1 C4 D5 E3.

23 **EW is Extinct in the Wild.** The species has disappeared in nature, although there may be a few surviving in zoos and wildlife parks. An example is the Hawaiian crow. The last two wild birds disappeared in 2002, although some live in cages. EX is Extinct, or gone forever. Usually this means the animal has not been seen for 50 years.

On the critical list

24 The most threatened animals in the world are CR, Critically Endangered. One of the most famous CR mammals is the mountain gorilla. There are just a few hundred left in the high peaks of Central Africa. They suffer from loss of their natural habitat, being killed for meat and trophies, and from catching human diseases.

▲ Smallest of the rhinos, at about 1,550 pounds, the Sumatran rhino is poached for its horns. These are powdered for use in traditional so-called "medicines."

25 The most threatened group of big mammals is the rhinos. Of the five species, three are CR—the Javan and Sumatran rhinos of Southeast Asia, and the black rhino of Africa. The Indian rhino is endangered, EN. They all suffer from loss of natural living areas and being killed for their horns.

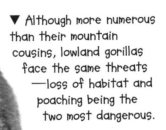

▼ Although more numerous than their mountain cousins, lowland gorillas face the same threats —loss of habitat and poaching being the two most dangerous.

MAKE A RHINO NOSE

You will need:
Large sheet of card   Sticky tape

A rhino's nose horn may be more than three feet long! Make your own by rolling some card into a cone shape and taping it firmly. Hold the "horn" angled up from your own nose. How do rhinos see where they are going?

26 The kouprey or Cambodian forest ox is another critical mammal. It has big horns and weighs more than one ton but there are probably fewer than 250 left in Southeast Asia. Apart from losing its natural habitat, the kouprey is hunted by local people and it catches diseases from farm cattle. It is also killed for food by soldiers who fight for local warlords and hide in the forest.

▲ The kouprey grazes on grasses by night and hides in the thick forest during the day.

▼ Right whales are slow swimmers and stay near the surface, which made them easy targets for whalers.

27 The northern right whale has never recovered from being slaughtered during the mass killing of whales in the last century. There are now probably less than 600 left. These whales breed so slowly that they may never increase in numbers.

28 Apart from big, well-known mammals, many other smaller mammal species are on the critical list. They include the hispid hare (Assam rabbit) and dwarf blue sheep of the Himalaya Mountains, and the northern hairy-nosed wombat of northeast Australia.

All kinds under threat

29 Mammals such as pandas, whales, and tigers are not the only endangered animals—there are many other threatened species from all animal groups. Among the birds is the Bermuda petrel, the national seabird of the island of Bermuda. Only about 250 survive and the islanders are making a huge conservation effort to help them.

▲ The young Bermuda petrel stays at sea for about five years before it comes back to land to breed.

30 A critical reptile is the Batagur baska (river turtle or terrapin) of India and Southeast Asia. One reason for its rarity was that people collected its eggs, especially in Cambodia, to give as presents to the king. King Norodom Sihamoni of Cambodia has now given orders to protect the baska.

▼ The batagur "royal turtle" grows to more than three feet long and 65 pounds in weight. It eats all kinds of foods, from plants to fish and crabs.

31 An endangered amphibian is Hamilton's frog of New Zealand. It is perhaps the rarest frog in the world. Hamilton's frog does not croak, does not have webbed feet, and hatches from its egg not as a tadpole, but as a fully formed froglet.

▼ The Devil's Hole pupfish is one of several very rare fish, each found in one small pool.

▲ Hamilton's frog is less than 2 inches long. There may be as few as 300 left in the wild.

32 A fish that is vulnerable (VU) is the Devil's Hole pupfish. It lives naturally in just one warm pool, Devil's Hole, in a limestone cave in the desert near Death Valley, USA. There are usually around 200–400 pupfish there, but after problems with floods and droughts, the number by 2006 was less than 50.

Male

33 One of the rarest insects is the Queen Alexandra's birdwing butterfly. It lives in a small area on the island of Papua New Guinea. In 1950, a nearby volcano erupted and destroyed much of the butterfly's forest habitat, so it is now endangered (EN).

▶ Like many tropical butterflies, the female and male Queen Alexandra's birdwing look quite different from each other.

I DON'T BELIEVE IT!
The Bermuda petrel was thought to be extinct for over 300 years until a breeding group was discovered on some coastal rocks in 1951.

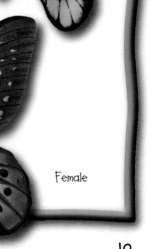
Female

The greatest threat

34 Endangered animals face dozens of different threats, but the greatest problem for most of them is habitat loss. This means the wild places or natural habitats where they live are being changed or destroyed, so animals, plants, and other wildlife can no longer survive there.

35 Habitat loss is not a new threat—it has been happening for thousands of years. Across much of Europe, farmland for crops and livestock gradually replaced once-great woods and forests. This meant the disappearance of forest animals such as bears, wild boars, wolves, and beavers.

36 Today, habitat loss is happening at a terrifying rate, especially for tropical forests. These forests are "hot spots" that have the richest range of wildlife, known as biodiversity. They occur mainly in Central and South America, West Africa, and Southeast Asia—and this is where most endangered animals live.

37 The muriquis or wooly spider monkeys of Brazil are critically endangered. Trees in their tropical forests have been chopped down for logs and the timber trade. Then the land is cleared for farm animals and crops. The monkeys, along with thousands of other forest species, have fewer places to live.

▼ Tropical forests are chopped down for their valuable hardwoods such as teak and mahogany. What remains is burnt and the land cleared for crops.

38 In Borneo, animals from pygmy elephants to orangutans are under threat as their forests are cleared for oil palm trees and other crops. Oil palm plantations are one of the main reasons for habitat loss across the tropics. The vegetable oil from the fleshy fruits is used for cooking, to make margarine and prepared meals, and for a vehicle fuel known as biodiesel.

Too many people

39 Many animals no longer live in their natural habitats because people now live there. The number of people in the world increases by about 150 every minute. They need houses, land for farms, shops, schools, factories, and roads. More people means less places for wildlife.

40 Animals living in lakes, rivers, marshes, and swamps are some of the most endangered. Their habitats are drained and cleared for towns, ports, and waterside holiday centers. Tourist areas along rivers and coastlines endanger all kinds of animals.

▼ Across the world, cities spread into nearby natural habitats, such as this shanty town in Colombia, South America.

QUIZ

Can you name the major threats these animals face?
1. Mediterranean monk seal
2. Red panda
3. Black-necked crane
4. Golden bamboo lemur

Answers:
1. Spread of holiday areas along the Mediterranean 2. Loss of bamboo 3. Tourists 4. Loss of trees in Madagascar due to spreading villages and farms

41 The Mediterranean monk seal has suffered greatly from the spread of tourism. Its breeding and resting areas have been taken over for holiday villages, sunbathing beaches, and water sports. This seal has also been hunted by fishermen, who believe it "steals" their fish, and affected by pollution. It is now critical, with fewer than 600 left.

▲ The shy Mediterranean monk seal is frightened by boats and divers, and tries to hide in underwater caves.

42 The black-necked crane lives in the highlands around the Himalayas in Asia. It faces several threats. One is the development of tourism in a region known as the Ladakh Valley in India. People come to gaze at the marvelous scenery and watch the wildlife, but they disturb the cranes, who are shy and less likely to breed.

▶ Black-necked cranes are sometimes poisoned by pesticide chemicals used by farmers.

43 The giant panda is a famous rare animal, and its distant cousin, the red panda, is also under threat. This tree-dwelling bamboo-eater from South and East Asia has fewer places to live, as towns and villages spread quickly. It's also hunted for its fur, especially its bushy tail, which is used to make hats and good luck wedding charms.

▶ The red panda is fully protected by law, but hunting continues for its fur.

Pollution problems

44 Pollution is a threat to all wildlife, as the wastes and chemicals we make get into the air, soil, and water. Like many dangers to animals, pollution is often combined with other threats, such as habitat loss and climate change. Sometimes it is difficult to separate these dangers, since one is part of another.

▲ This Atlantic croaker fish has become blind with misty eyes, or cataracts, due to chemicals in the water.

45 Harmful chemicals spread quickly through water to affect streams, rivers, lakes, and even the open ocean. Caspian seals live in the landlocked Caspian Sea, a vast lake in West Asia. Industries and factories around the lake shore pollute its waters. The seals suffer from sores and fur loss, and are less resistant to diseases.

◀ Oil spillages are a devastating form of pollution. This beaver is covered in oil, which it tries to lick from its coat. By doing so it swallows poisonous chemicals that may kill it.

46 The largest amphibians in the world are Chinese and Japanese giant salamanders. They are in danger from pollution of their cool, fast-flowing, highland streams. There are few factories there, but the clouds and rains carry polluting chemicals from the smoke and fumes of factory chimneys far away.

POLLUTION HAZARDS

Next time you are in the park or countryside, look out for types of pollution. Find out how they could harm animals, and how we can reduce them. Look for examples such as:

Litter in ponds • Plastic bags in bushes and hedges • Pools of oil or fuel from vehicles Broken glass • Pipes carrying poisonous liquids into ditches, streams, or rivers • Metal wire, plastic tags, and similar objects

▼ The baiji's home in the Yangtze River has become a dangerous, polluted place. The last sighting of one of these dolphins was in 2004.

47 A survey in 2006 failed to find any baijis, or Chinese river dolphins. One of the threats to this dolphin is pollution of its main river, the Yangtze or Chang Jiang, by factories along its banks, and by farm chemicals seeping into the water from fields. The pollution has harmed not only the baiji but also the fish and other animals that it eats. Further threats include hunting by people for its meat, the building of dams, drowning in fishing nets, and being hit by boats.

Baiji (Chinese river dolphin)

48 **The whole world faces climate change, which could endanger many animal species.** The weather is gradually becoming warmer because our atmosphere (the layer of air around Earth) is being altered by "greenhouse gases." These come mainly from burning fuels such as petrol, diesel, wood, coal, and natural gas. They make the Earth trap heat from the Sun, and so the planet gets hotter.

▶ Penguins become tired after feeding in the water for several hours, and need to rest on the shore or an iceberg. Global warming means that the ice is melting and penguins' resting places are disappearing.

50 **In the far south, penguins have trouble finding icebergs to rest on.** As in the north, the icebergs melt faster due to global warming. Like the polar bears, the penguins cannot get out of the water for a rest, and because they cannot fly, they may drown.

49 **In the far north, polar bears are threatened because ice floes (big lumps of ice) are melting faster.** The bears use the ice floes to hunt seals from and to rest on. There used to be plenty of floes, but now polar bears can swim for hours before finding one. Some bears even drown, exhausted in the open sea.

▶ Fewer, smaller ice floes spell terrible trouble for polar bears.

51 Global warming is changing the seasons, which may affect huge numbers of animals. An earlier spring means that insects in Europe breed a week or two before they used to. However, migrating birds from Africa, such as pied flycatchers, swallows, and swifts, might arrive too late to catch the insects for their chicks. Scientists call this "uncoupling" of the natural links between animals and their seasonal food.

52 The huge Asian fish, the beluga sturgeon, is already endangered. It is poached for the female's eggs, which are sold as the expensive food caviar. However, as global warming continues, the sturgeon's rivers and lakes will be affected, which could push the fish to extinction even more quickly.

I DON'T BELIEVE IT!

Scientists studying 40,000 tree swallows say that the birds now lay their eggs nine days earlier than they did 40 years ago, probably as a result of global warming.

▲ Beluga sturgeons used to grow to more than 16 feet long, but most of them are now caught and killed before they reach such a great size or age.

Poaching and souvenirs

◄ Weight for weight, rhino horn can be worth more than gems such as rubies and pearls.

54 The main reason that rhinos are so endangered is because of poaching for their horns. The horns are carved into decorative objects such as dagger handles, or ground down to make traditional Chinese medicine. The most common use is to bring down fevers—although there is little scientific proof this works.

53 Some animals are endangered because they are hunted for trophies, souvenirs, and body parts. Poaching is the illegal killing of animals for their body parts, such as elephants for their ivory tusks.

MATCH UP

Can you match the animals with the products they are killed or captured for?

A. Tiger
B. Elephant
C. Giant clam
D. Rhino

1. Dagger handle
2. Tourist souvenir
3. Bones
4. Ivory

Answers:
A3 B4 C2 D1

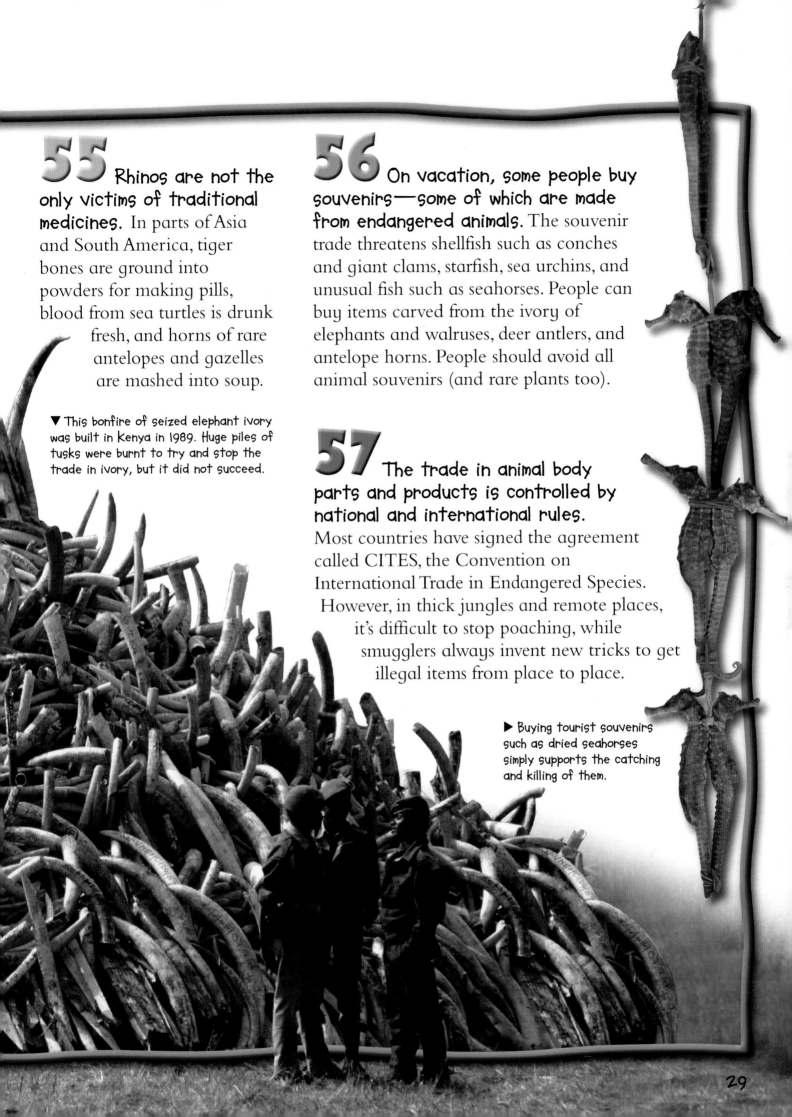

55 Rhinos are not the only victims of traditional medicines. In parts of Asia and South America, tiger bones are ground into powders for making pills, blood from sea turtles is drunk fresh, and horns of rare antelopes and gazelles are mashed into soup.

▼ This bonfire of seized elephant ivory was built in Kenya in 1989. Huge piles of tusks were burnt to try and stop the trade in ivory, but it did not succeed.

56 On vacation, some people buy souvenirs—some of which are made from endangered animals. The souvenir trade threatens shellfish such as conches and giant clams, starfish, sea urchins, and unusual fish such as seahorses. People can buy items carved from the ivory of elephants and walruses, deer antlers, and antelope horns. People should avoid all animal souvenirs (and rare plants too).

57 The trade in animal body parts and products is controlled by national and international rules. Most countries have signed the agreement called CITES, the Convention on International Trade in Endangered Species. However, in thick jungles and remote places, it's difficult to stop poaching, while smugglers always invent new tricks to get illegal items from place to place.

▶ Buying tourist souvenirs such as dried seahorses simply supports the catching and killing of them.

Kill or be killed

58 Some animals are endangered because of the threat they pose to people—at least, that is the belief. Big, powerful predators are seen as dangerous to people, pets, and farm animals. The risk of possible attack leads to persecution and revenge killing of the animal species. Hunters become the hunted.

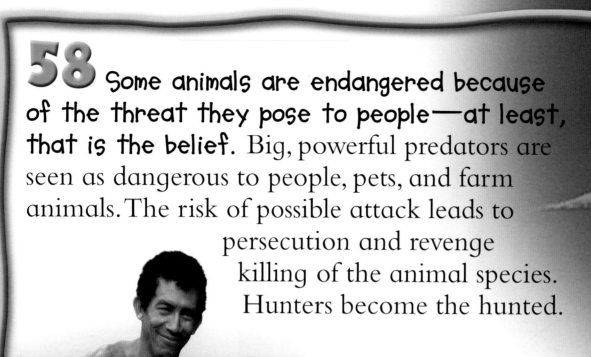

59 In Central and South America, the jaguar, a spotted big cat, is often killed because of the risk that it might attack farm animals. Large areas of forest are cleared for cattle grazing, and some ranchers hire professional jaguar hunters who shoot the big cats on sight. Jaguars used to be killed for another reason—their beautiful fur coats. However, trade in jaguar fur and other body parts is now illegal.

◀ In parts of South America, hunters kill small crocodiles called caimans to sell their skins and flesh, even though it's against the law.

60 Crocodiles and alligators are shot because of the threats they pose to people and their animals. The endangered Cuban crocodile lives in only a small region of rivers and swamps on the Caribbean island of Cuba. It is a small crocodile, about 6.5 to 8 feet long. However, it has long been hunted because of the danger of attack, as well as for its meat and skin.

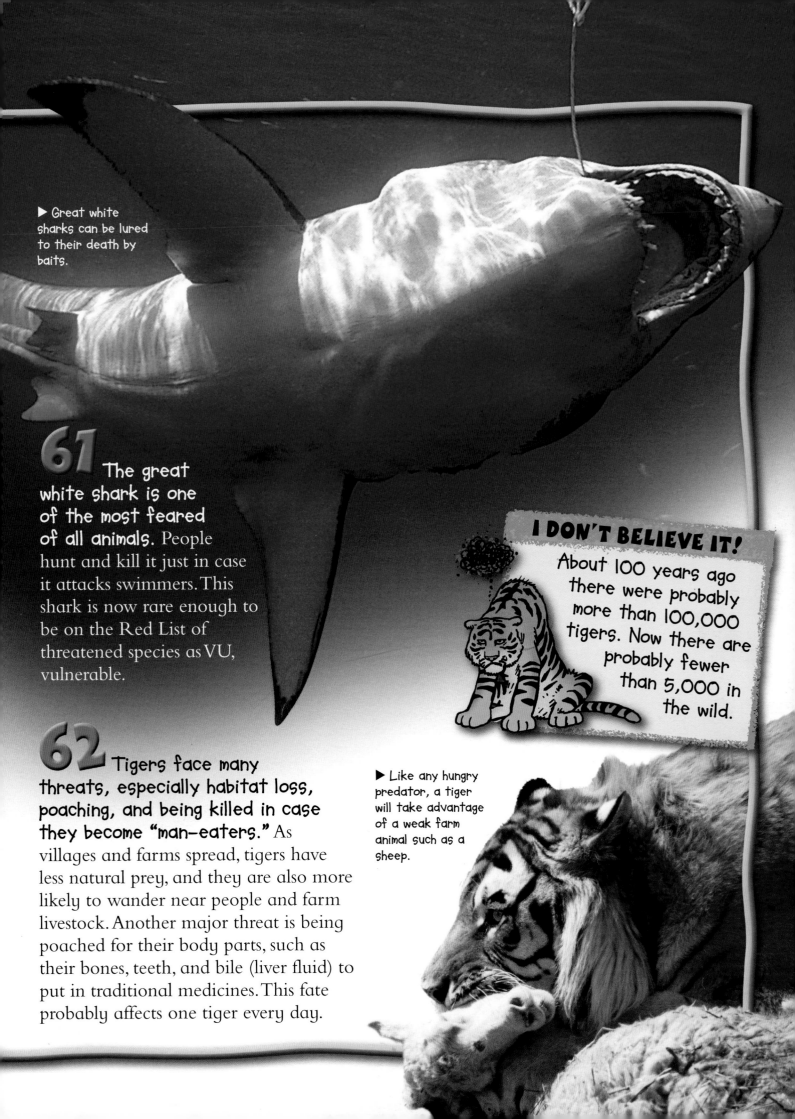

► Great white sharks can be lured to their death by baits.

61 The great white shark is one of the most feared of all animals. People hunt and kill it just in case it attacks swimmers. This shark is now rare enough to be on the Red List of threatened species as VU, vulnerable.

62 Tigers face many threats, especially habitat loss, poaching, and being killed in case they become "man-eaters." As villages and farms spread, tigers have less natural prey, and they are also more likely to wander near people and farm livestock. Another major threat is being poached for their body parts, such as their bones, teeth, and bile (liver fluid) to put in traditional medicines. This fate probably affects one tiger every day.

► Like any hungry predator, a tiger will take advantage of a weak farm animal such as a sheep.

63 The bushmeat trade—hunting wild animals for food—is a growing threat to many species. People have always ventured into the forest to kill wild animals to eat. However modern rifles, traps, and other weapons mean that more animals can be caught, and sold at market. This growing trade in commercial bushmeat has become a huge problem.

▲ Bushmeat is sold at many local markets such as this one in West Africa. Once the animals have been skinned and cut up, it's difficult to identify if they are protected.

64 In Africa, the drill and mandrill are the world's largest monkeys, and both are in huge danger from the bushmeat trade. Killing one of these animals and selling most of its meat provides enough money to buy a week's food for a family.

▼ For thousands of years, local people have caught and eaten animals, such as this monkey, from the forests around them.

I DON'T BELIEVE IT!

The blackbuck antelope is protected in India. It was introduced to the US, and it breeds so well on ranches that numbers have to be reduced. So it's eaten in restaurants, and spare blackbucks are sent back to India to keep up the numbers.

▶ Near Lake Turkana in East Africa, villagers have caught and killed a hippo—bushmeat hunting can be very dangerous for people, too.

65

In West Africa, the pygmy hippo is endangered due to hunting for its meat. This small hippo lives in thick forests and travels along regular tracks to and from its feeding areas. If hunters find a track, they lie in wait for their prey. Fewer than 3,000 pygmy hippos are left in the wild.

66

Mainly in India, and through most of Southeast Asia, bushmeat hunting is affecting more animals. The thamin, or Eld's deer, is listed as VU, vulnerable. In some places they have so little forest left that they eat farm crops. Local people kill them to stop the crop damage—and to have a meal.

67

In South America, the Brazilian tapir's flesh is considered a delicacy, so it is a prize target for bushmeat hunters. It is VU, vulnerable, but its cousin, the mountain tapir, is even more at risk. There are less than 2,500 in the wild and better protection is needed.

▲ In West Africa, logging vehicles leaving the forest are checked for animals captured for the bushmeat trade.

Threats for pets

68 Some animals are endangered because they are caught from the wild to become pets or captives. There is a thriving illegal trade in supplying rare animals as pets, and to personal collectors and private zoos. It is not only illegal but also cruel and wasteful. Many of the animals suffer and die on the long journeys to their new homes.

▲ Exotic pets, such as this macaw, often travel in terrible conditions, cramped and dirty, with little or no food and water. They end up in cages where they often die.

▼ Criminals dig up and steal the eggs of the Komodo dragon, which fetch large sums of money in the illegal collecting trade.

69 The world's biggest lizard, the endangered Komodo dragon, has its eggs stolen from the wild by thieves. These are sold to egg collectors, reptile breeders, and lizard fanciers. This is illegal, but some people cannot resist the thrill of having such a rare egg, even if they must keep it secret.

70 Colorful, clever birds such as parrots and macaws are sometimes caught for the caged bird trade, rather than being bred in captivity. Rare species such as the hyacinth macaw, the biggest of all the parrots, and the green-winged macaw, are taken from the wild. It is against the law, but bird collectors pay huge amounts for them.

QUIZ

1. What is the world's biggest lizard?
2. Why is this lizard endangered?
3. What is the world's biggest parrot?
4. What is the world's biggest frog?

Answers:
1. Komodo dragon 2. Because people steal its eggs to sell 3. Hyacinth macaw 4. Goliath frog

◄ This tilapia cichlid fish has been caught from the wild and placed in an aquarium. It has a burn mark on its back from resting too near to the aquarium lights.

71 Various tropical fish are caught from rivers and lakes for the aquarium trade. Some of the rarest are the tilapia cichlid fishes of the African Rift Valley lakes. Responsible aquarium suppliers and respected pet stores know about threatened species and do not accept those caught in the wild.

72 The world's biggest frog, the Goliath frog of Africa, is taken from the wild and sold to amphibian fanciers and private collectors. Its head and body are 12 inches long, and it can leap 20 feet in one jump. Being so large, this frog is also a good catch for the bushmeat trade.

▶ In West Africa, Goliath frogs—classed as endangered, EN—are caught in nets or traps. Their numbers are thought to have halved in the past 20 years.

Island problems

73 **Many threatened animals live on islands.** Here, the creatures and plants have lived together for many years. They have changed, or evolved, to become specialized to their unique habitat. The small size of many islands means less animals, and the unique habitat is easily upset when people arrive.

▲ Each type of Galapagos Island finch, including this mangrove finch, has evolved a beak shape suited to eating certain kinds of food.

Mangrove finch

74 **The mangrove finch, which lives on the Galapagos Islands in the Pacific Ocean, is critically endangered.** It is one of Darwin's finches—the birds that helped English naturalist Charles Darwin (1809–1882) work out his theory of evolution, which is so important to science.

75 **Also on the Galapagos, giant tortoises are under threat, partly due to a common island problem— introduced species.** People have taken many animals to islands, such as cats, rats, rabbits, and dogs. These new arrivals destroy the natural habitat, prey on some local species, and compete for food and shelter.

▶ "Lonesome George" is the last of his kind —a Pinta Island giant Galapagos tortoise. When he dies, the species will no longer exist.

76 The island of Madagascar has amazing and unique wildlife, but much of it is in danger. Lemurs, such as the ring-tailed lemur, are found nowhere else in the wild. However, many Madagascan species are threatened by a mixture of habitat loss, hunting for food, capture for the illegal pet trade, and the problem of introduced species.

◄ Ring-tailed lemurs are popular in wildlife parks and zoos, but are becoming rarer on their island home of Madagascar.

77 On islands, not just exciting species such as giant tortoises and colorful birds are threatened. There are less glamorous species, such as the partula snails of the South Pacific islands. They were eaten by a predatory snail called Euglandina, which was introduced to provide food for local people.

78 There have been more than 700 known animal extinctions in the last 400 years—and about half of these were on islands. In the Hawaiian islands alone about 25 kinds of birds, 70 types of snails, 80 kinds of insects, and more than 100 plants have disappeared in the past 200 years.

► Some species of partula snails now survive only in zoos or science laboratories.

Stop the slaughter

79 For more than 50 years there has been a growing awareness of endangered animals and how we can save them. "Headline" species such as pandas, whales, tigers, and gorillas grab the interest of people and help to raise money for conservation. This conservation work can then protect natural habitats and so save many other species as well.

▲ The Born Free Foundation is an international wildlife charity working around the world to protect threatened species in the wild.

80 In the 1960s, the giant panda of China became famous as the symbol of the World Wildlife Fund, WWF (now World Wide Fund for Nature). Huge conservation efforts mean the giant panda is now off the critical list, with some 2,000 in the wild, although it is still listed as EN, endangered.

◀ Pandas eat almost nothing but particular kinds of bamboo, so they rely heavily on their specialized habitat.

I DON'T BELIEVE IT!

The giant panda was chosen as a symbol of conservation partly because of its black-and-white colors. These make its image easier to photocopy without the need for any colors.

81 In the 1970s, people started to protest against the commercial hunting of great whales, which was threatening many whale species. "Save the Whale" campaigns and marches became popular. Eventually in 1980 there was a world ban on the mass hunting of large whales.

83 In the 1990s, the terrible crisis facing the tiger became clear. Save the Tiger Fund was founded in 1995 to fight the many dangers facing the biggest of big cats. However, it is too late for some varieties, or subspecies, of tiger. The Balinese tiger from the island of Bali became extinct in the 1930s, and the Javan tiger followed in the 1980s.

82 In the 1980s, there were many anti-fur campaigns, to stop the killing of wild cats and other animals for their fur coats. This helped to reduce one of the threats to many beautiful cat species, not only big cats, but also medium and small species such as the ocelot and margay. Sadly, fur is becoming a popular fashion item once more.

▶ Great whales, such as these blue whales, are now fairly safe from mass slaughter. However, they breed very slowly and their numbers will take many years to start rising again.

A place to live

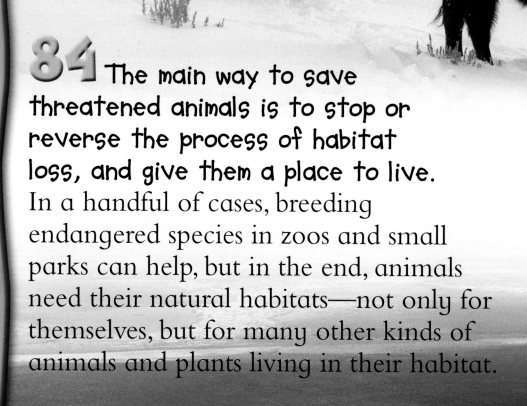

84 The main way to save threatened animals is to stop or reverse the process of habitat loss, and give them a place to live. In a handful of cases, breeding endangered species in zoos and small parks can help, but in the end, animals need their natural habitats—not only for themselves, but for many other kinds of animals and plants living in their habitat.

▲ Bison were just saved from extinction and now roam freely in Yellowstone, Wood Buffalo, and other North American parks.

▼ The Great Barrier Reef Marine Park has gradually been extended over the years, with limited tourism in some areas and complete protection in others.

85 Natural places are preserved by setting aside large areas as national parks, nature reserves, and wildlife sanctuaries. In 1872, Yellowstone National Park became the world's first national park. As in other protected areas, there are laws preventing people from damaging the animals, plants, or habitat. Yellowstone's animals include the American bison or "buffalo," which used to roam the prairies in millions. It almost became extinct in the 1880s but was just saved.

86 Some of the most important and precious wild areas are given the title of World Heritage Site. In Ethiopia, East Africa, the Simien National Park is home to extremely rare animals such as the gelada baboon, the Ethiopian wolf (Simien fox or jackal), and a type of wild goat called the Walia ibex, of which there are only 500 left.

▲ The 500 surviving Ethiopian wolves are found in only a few areas, such as the Bale Mountains and Simien National Park in Ethiopia.

87 One of the world's biggest protected ocean areas is Australia's Great Barrier Reef Marine Park, home to amazing animals from tiny coral creatures to huge sharks. In 2006 the US set up the even bigger NorthWest Hawaiian Island National Monument. This reserve is home to more than 7,000 animal species including the threatened Hawaiian monk seal, green turtle, and Laysan albatross.

Captive breeding

88 Zoos, wildlife parks, and breeding centers may play an important role in saving animals. Some animals are kept and encouraged to breed and build up their numbers, hopefully for release back into the wild. This method needs expert knowledge about the species, so the zoo keepers can look after the animals well. However, it can only be used in selected cases.

89 Not only big exciting animals are bred in captivity—one of the smallest is the Chatham Island black robin. By the early 1980s, only five remained, with just one female, "Old Blue." Careful captive breeding involved taking away her first batch of eggs, so she would lay a second clutch, while keepers cared for the first batch so they hatched. There are now more than 250 black robins.

▼ When rare animals such as the giant panda are reared in captivity, scientists can learn much about them.

◀ Pere David's deer have been released back into their home area of China.

90 For many years, Pere David's deer lived only in reserves owned by the emperors of China. Gradually the deer disappeared—many were eaten. However, a few were taken to Woburn animal park in the UK, where they bred. In the 1980s, some Pere David's deer were released back into the wild in China, where they are still CR, critically endangered.

▼ Blue Iguanas are tagged so they can be closely monitored in their protected areas.

91 The critically endangered Grand Cayman Blue Iguana was down to fewer than 15 lizards. Since 1996, captive-bred lizards have been released into protected areas on the island of Grand Cayman, and more reserves and releases are planned.

▼ Tigers breed well in some zoos, but release into the wild is virtually impossible. Captive tigers lose their instinct to kill, so may starve to death.

92 There are many problems when releasing captive-bred animals back into the wild, especially for apes such as orangutans. Young apes learn from their parents about how to find food and avoid danger. If they are brought up in captivity they may need to be taught by people how to become wild again.

93 Many endangered animals face a variety of threats, so helping them needs a variety of actions, all organized into a conservation program. For example, it is little use providing a wildlife park for a rare bird if the park is overrun with rats that will eat the bird's eggs.

▶ The Arabian oryx seemed to be recovering its numbers, but these are falling again.

94 By 1972 the last wild Arabian oryx, a gazelle from the Middle East, had been killed. However, some oryx had been captured and bred, especially in Phoenix Zoo, USA. A reserve was set up in Oman in the Middle East and 10 captive-bred oryx were released there in 1981. Their numbers rose. However in 2007, Oman reduced the reserve's size. Oryx numbers have since fallen from over 400 to less than 70.

MAKE A CONDOR PUPPET!

You will need:
Old sock   Paints and paintbrush

A Californian condor chick takes food from its parent. So conservation workers "trick the chick" by making parent look-alike puppets. Paint an old sock with the colors shown to make a pretend condor head. Would you take food from it?

▶ Pygmy hogs are about 12 inches tall and weigh just 22 pounds. They were once widespread along the southern foothills of the Himalaya Mountains, in marshes and swamps with tall grasses.

95
The Californian condor is a huge bird of prey from southwest North America. Its numbers fell over many years due to habitat loss, poaching, poisoning from eating animals killed by lead shot from guns or pesticide chemicals, and even crashing into power lines. In 1987, all 22 known condors were captured for breeding at Los Angeles Zoo and San Diego Wild Animal Park. Gradually numbers increased. By the mid 2000s there were more than 250 birds, including more than 100 back in the wild.

96
The pygmy hog of the Indian region is CR, critically endangered. There are probably less than 200 left, mainly due to loss of their natural habitat for farming, and also being killed for food. One of their last areas is the Manas Tiger Reserve in the Assam region. In 1995, the Pygmy Hog Conservation Programme was founded to help this unusual type of pig to survive.

◀ Californian condors are big enough to carry radio tracking devices, so scientists can study how far they fly, and where they feed and nest.

Future help

▼ Whale-watching not only helps people to appreciate the wonders of these great animals, but also how important it is to save all natural places and their wildlife.

97 **Saving threatened animals is not just for wildlife organizations and governments —everyone can help.** You could volunteer for a conservation group, or set up a wildlife club in your school or neighborhood. You might raise awareness by telling family and friends about threatened species, or have a "rare animals" birthday party.

98 **Local zoos and wildlife parks often have lots of information about endangered animals and their conservation.** You can visit, write, or email them, to ask if they are involved in conservation. Find out how zoos share information about their rare animals, so suitable individuals can be brought together for breeding. Wildlife conservation organizations often offer animal adoptions so you can sponsor a rare animal, maybe as a birthday present or a gift.

99 **Saving threatened animals cannot be done without saving their habitats —and taking into account people.** The people who live in the same area as a rare species may be very poor and very hungry. They see lots of time and money being spent on the endangered animal, but nothing for themselves.

100 Countries and governments must take into account their people, animals, plants, and habitats, for a long-term and sustainable result. For example, wildlife can help to raise money by encouraging environmentally responsible tourism. This is when people pay to see rare creatures, such as gorillas, whales, and tigers, under careful, monitored conditions. Then the money is used for local conservation that helps people as well as wildlife. Only in this way can people and endangered animals live together for the future.

I DON'T BELIEVE IT!

In 2005, a new kind of monkey, the highland mangabey, was discovered in Africa. At the same time it became one of the rarest and most threatened of all animal species.

▶ A close-up view of a tiger can encourage tourists to support campaigns to save these beautiful animals, and thereby protect large areas of their habitat for other creatures and plants.

Index

Entries in **bold** refer to main subject entries. Entries in *italics* refer to illustrations.